Zingerman's
community of businesses

statement
of beliefs

Zingerman's ® community of businesses
statement of beliefs

what we believe alters what happens at work every day

Zingerman's
PRESS
ann arbor, mi

contents

ZINGERMAN'S STATEMENT OF BELIEFS

©2021 DSE INC.
First edition, 2021

Please direct requests for permission to
ZINGERMAN'S PRESS
3756 Plaza Dr.
Ann Arbor, MI 48108
zingermanspress.com

Printed, bound, and warehoused in Michigan

ISBN 978-0-9893494-1-3

BOOK DESIGN & PRODUCTION
Patrick Barber
Sasha Zein

EDITOR
Jenny Tubbs

**COVER ILLUSTRATIONS
& LETTERING**
Ian Nagy

SPOT ILLUSTRATIONS
Ian Nagy
Ryan Stiner

Set in Meno Text, Meno Display,
and Proxima Nova

a little context

introduction

ONE OF THE THINGS that became clear to me in writing *A Lapsed Anarchist's Approach to the Power of Beliefs in Business* is that organizations would benefit greatly from getting clear alignment on the key beliefs that underlie the way the business runs. As with everything else we do, we know that if we have a shared understanding and agreed-upon approaches to our work, our decision-making will get easier, our hiring and training will be more effective, things will flow more smoothly, and waste will be reduced. As author Kevin Bermingham puts it: "Beliefs are simply a feeling of conviction or certainty that something is real or true. They're based on our past experiences and what others have taught us. Beliefs are our best guess at reality—our mental model of how the world appears to work … Our knowledge of the real world is limited. So to get by, we rely on our beliefs instead. They're the principles and rules by which we assume the world works."

This booklet offers a look at how we are committing to put our shared organizational beliefs to work every day here at Zingerman's. In the pages that follow, you'll find a listing of the Compelling Reasons for creating the Statement of Beliefs, as well as our Vision for how the Statement of Beliefs will play out positively in the coming years. You'll see a series of definitions for key terms we use. In the center spread, you'll find two pages that list beliefs to which we've committed ourselves to living (if you want to get to the heart of the matter, just jump to page 12 right now). In the second half of the booklet, we share practical and detailed day-to-day examples of what each of those beliefs looks like in action—both when we're living them well, and then, also when we fall short. Lastly, there's a page for notes and reflections to help you track what all these means to you.

Thank you for all the work you've done—as a staff member, customer, or supplier—to help make the imperfect ecosystem of the Zingerman's Community of Businesses what it is today. And thank you for working so hard—in part by diligently living these beliefs every day—to make it even better still as we move, slowly but surely, towards our 2032 Vision. We hope it helps make your experience here at Zingerman's more rewarding. Because, as we say in the Statement, "We believe good work can be one of the most fulfilling things one ever engages in."

bottom-Line change steps 1 & 2 for the statement of beliefs

Bottom-Line Change® (BLC) is our 5-step recipe for organizational change. It's our process for introducing new changes into the ZCoB. Here are Steps 1 and 2 as we used them in 2019 and 2020 to help roll out the Statement of Beliefs.

STEP 1

Compelling reasons for writing a Statement of Beliefs for the ZCoB

- Actions we take are based on what we believe.

- Most of us are not cognizant of our beliefs.

- If we have unacknowledged conflicting beliefs, we will end up in conflict.

- Our Training Compact talks our commitment to provide clear expectations. The Statement of Beliefs is a very helpful tool for doing that.

- When expectations about our beliefs are clear, we will be much more inclusive of new co-workers—they can quickly come up to speed on the "cultural norms" by which we work every day in the ZCoB.

- When beliefs are in the open and available for applicants to consider, they can decide in advance if they want to work with those beliefs.

- A statement of beliefs with clear "in alignment" and "out of alignment" examples that's actively shared, is a valuable training tool.

- The statement of beliefs is a great way to "Provide training resources" and the "training tools" we all need to succeed.

- If we have agreed-upon beliefs, it will make it easier to make effective decisions.

- Once we have a shared statement of beliefs, we can much more productively use Bottom-Line Change to make changes to those beliefs when appropriate

- The more we familiarize ourselves with the Self-Fulfilling-Belief Cycle the more productive our conversations can be around difficult issues and the more effective we can ll be in self-management.

Vision of our Statement of Beliefs in action

It's February of 2023, and we're heading to the twentieth partner offsite. The ZCoB Statement of Beliefs has been solidly in place for over three years now, and it's helped us to be an ever more effective organization. What were once often unspoken, below the surface ideas and approaches, are now much more clearly laid out for all to see, read, and think about. In the same way that our values, mission, and vision have helped us become drastically more effective in our decision-making and in our work over the last few decades, our Statement of Beliefs now contributes positively in much the same way. When we're struggling with what to do, we can refer back to it to get re-grounded. It's helped with hiring—just as our vision and values help us to filter applicants, and help applicants decide if we're a good fit for them, the Statement of Beliefs does much the same thing. Progressive thinkers are drawn to the positive nature of our beliefs and feel empowered and encouraged by them. It helps with training—our organizational expectations are clearer which reduces stress and helps everyone succeed. The Statement of Beliefs—added to our governance work—has helped with succession planning and preparation. Others around the country are now following our lead. The process of writing belief statements is now something that ZingTrain gets regular inquiries about. As with so many of the processes and constructs we believe in—Visioning, The 3 Steps to Great Service, Open-Book management, LEAN—it's made us a better business, and indirectly, brought in business at the same time. Having our Statement of Beliefs helped enormously when we wrote the next long-term vision for 2032.

Because beliefs are freely chosen and can be changed when appropriate, we revisit our Statement of Beliefs and adjust accordingly. Like all major documents, a change can be initiated by anyone, and is given final approval by the Partner's Group. Last year we already made two or three adjustments. Early in 2022 we also revisited our Guiding Principles and made some adjustments there—a few things left the Guiding Principles and now reside on our Statement of Beliefs. A few things that were informally but very strongly held, ethically important beliefs were added to our Guiding Principles. Beliefs now show up on the Business Perspective Chart in order to help keep common language throughout the ZCoB. Our work to get clear around beliefs has helped ZCoBbers to give more consideration to their own beliefs and in the process that work has helped many here to enhance the quality of their own lives.

the belief cycle

Excerpt from *Zingerman's Guide to Good Leading, Part 4: A Lapsed Anarchist's Approach to The Power of Beliefs in Business.*

If you take the word "belief" and swap around the second "e" and the "f," you get "be life": our beliefs are the basis for the way our lives are going and are going to go in the future.

Whether we realize it or not, what we believe in our heads is highly likely to happen in the world around us. Good beliefs often beget good outcomes. If we believe things are going to be bad, it's likely that they will be. In which case it will be as authors Bob and Judith Wright tell us in their very fine book *Transformed!*: "In fact, what we believe limits our reality and keeps us from realizing our potential. We think, This is how it is, this is who I am, rather than This is how I'm programmed, this is what I believe, but it is not necessarily the full truth. It causes us to believe, I can't be assertive like that or I'm kind and thoughtful; I can't be angry."

Let me elaborate with a visual model that I learned from the Wrights. I give them full credit for the construct, and I share it here with their permission and active support (and my recommendation to buy their books and check out their work at the Wright Institute in Chicago). It connected for me as soon as I read it, and it has already helped thousands of others that we've shared it with here at work and through ZingTrain.

It works like this: When we have a belief, it's likely that belief will lead us to take some sort of associated action. For instance, let's say we believe that our ideas aren't worth much and no one really cares about what we think. The action that follows might be that we rarely voice our views at work. That behavior will likely feed the belief in others that we have little to offer, or perhaps aren't very committed to the company's success. Which will then lead those coworkers to take action accordingly—they might not ask us for our views on important issues or include us in discussions. Which will then reinforce our original belief that others don't value our views.

The cycle will surely continue onward from there. Imagine what it will feel like after 20 or 30 years. We start to believe that the reality we're experiencing is "who we are" rather than a result of how our beliefs have been acting steadily—if surreptitiously—on our reality. We know from studies of brain change and development that when we think in a certain way for a long period of time, the "routes" in our brain grow ever more deeply embedded. The deeper they get, the more we follow along the same path onto which our beliefs long ago led us. And on and on the cycle goes, each element reinforcing the existing beliefs of others

Zingerman's® STATEMENT OF BELIEFS

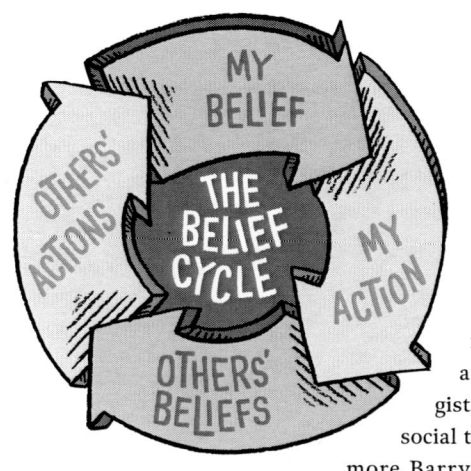

in the cycle. As author, psychologist, and professor of social theory at Swarthmore Barry Schwartz says, "These effects can arise because sometimes when people act on the basis of ideology, they inadvertently arrange the very conditions that bring reality into correspondence with the ideology."

All of which made clear to me how we each contribute to our own crises—both of conscience and of construct. It showed me that if I was frustrated with an action taken by others, I would do well to look away from them and turn back instead to inspect my own beliefs about the subject because, quite simply, our own beliefs are very often the cause of actions we don't like by others. Most importantly, it showed me that if I wanted to alter the outcomes I was getting in any situation, I would do well to begin by checking out my own beliefs about the other person, myself, and the world. Mindful effort, effective understanding, and consistent practice over an extended period of time can reverse the cycle. The change starts with a decision to adopt a new belief, or if you're thinking big, a whole new set of them.

In the scenario above, we might decide to change our belief by telling ourselves, "What I have to say does have value." Although it may be awkward and difficult at first, we start to act on this new belief. Rather than withhold our thoughts, we start to constructively share with others. As we do, people begin to believe that we have more to offer than they might have originally thought. In turn, their new belief will change their actions—they now start to ask for our opinion more often. That action begins to impact what we believe about ourselves, and our self-image slowly but surely starts to improve. Over time, we might become one of the most well-thought-of thinkers in the group.

Just recognizing the nature of this simple cycle is incredibly powerful. Our beliefs lead us to take certain actions, which inform the beliefs of others, which lead them to almost always act in ways that reinforce our original beliefs. It's what Claude Bristol wrote over half a century ago in *The Magic of Believing*: "Every person is the creation of himself, the image of his own thinking and believing. As individuals think and believe, so they are."

definitions

We believe life and work go better when we have well-understood and shared terminology. Here are some key terms.

Mission Statement

Our "North Star," keeping us focused on the big picture—to bring a great experience to everyone we come in contact with.

> *We share the Zingerman's Experience*
> *Selling food that makes you happy*
> *Giving service that makes you smile*
> *In passionate pursuit of our mission*
> *Showing love and care in all our actions*
> *To enrich as many lives as we possibly can.*

Vision

What success looks like at a particular point in time, described with enough detail that we'll know when we've arrived. An aspirational, vivid picture of our preferred future. Vision informs our goal setting, decision-making, and our daily work.

Guiding Principles

How we want to work together and relate to each other, our guests, our suppliers, and our community—ways we choose to behave even if doing so causes a financial penalty. They are beliefs that are ethically based and typically take precedence over other, less values-driven beliefs. They are at the core of everything we do, and they guide us in our work.

1. Great Food!

2. Great Service!

3. A Great Place to Shop and Eat!

4. Solid Profits!

5. A Great Place to Work!

6. Strong Relationships!

7. A Place to Learn!

8. An Active Part of Our Community!

Statement of Beliefs

Our mental model of how the world works. Not all beliefs rise to the level of Guiding Principles. They clarify how we see the world and what is at the root of our successes and struggles. Examining beliefs help us take responsibility for what we see and experience in the world. Beliefs need to be examined and re-examined in light of evidence and experience. We can choose and change beliefs more easily than principles.

By getting agreement up front on our beliefs, we can streamline the way we work—as with BLC, there's more work to do up front, but things flow more smoothly downstream.

Systems

We have lots of systems at Zingerman's. Everything from written recipes to financial statements and a 1001 things in between. Our systems are set up in order to help deliver the most effective bottom-line results possible while staying true to our Guiding Principles. In choosing to work here we make a commitment to work according to those systems, or to work constructively to change and improve them.

Culture

The culture is the "way it really is." We know that despite our best efforts, systems are never implemented 100% of the time. It's a normal part of organizational life that systems and culture are always in conflict. When there are gaps between our systems and our culture, it is up to each of us to work to get them back into alignment.

Results on 3 Bottom Lines

We need to be able to measure our success and our progress every day, every week, every month. Our three bottom lines are how we do that. On a day-to-day basis we are here to do three major things: Great Food, Great Service, and Great Finance.

organizational impact

Having a Statement of Beliefs will help us work more effectively in many ways. Here are three key areas of impact.

1. It helps with decision making. While many decision-making moments we face are "gray" in nature, having agreement on our underlying beliefs has made it easier to make those decisions. We can refer to the statement of beliefs to be reminded of what we've committed to. The Statement of Beliefs has given newer staff more of a framework to help them when they're unsure of what to do and touch points for conversations they initiate with others in the ZCoB as they work on shaping those decisions.

2. It helps with hiring. Giving the Statement of Beliefs to applicants allows us another avenue to share what we're about here at Zingerman's. After reading, they may be more motivated than ever to come work here. Or, on the other hand, they may opt out of working with us because they don't agree with our beliefs. Or they may begin thinking about things that they hadn't previously considered, even before their actual employment starts.

In the context of the Training Compact, it's giving much clearer expectations to everyone when they begin their employment in the ZCoB.

3. It helps with training. Before the Statement of Beliefs was rolled out, new ZCoBbers would pick these beliefs up mostly in passing or in one-on-one conversations that might or might not happen. The Statement of Beliefs has made it easy to hand new staff, and new managers, a list of our key beliefs (along with stories to illustrate them) right when they begin. While certainly not everyone will read it and internalize it overnight, the Statement of Beliefs does offer a positive tool to help disseminate this information more effectively and more tangibly—in other words, it can move us away from having this be mostly "culturally and behaviorally" communicated to making it overt and clear. We also live Servant Leadership more effectively by helping staff succeed here.

the statement

We believe leading with positive beliefs makes a positive difference. **PAGE 14**

We believe each person is a creative, unique individual who can do great things in life. **15**

We believe our individual success can be assessed by how much we help those around us to develop and grow. **16**

We believe personal transformation and growth are imperative to our personal and organizational success. **17**

We believe everyone can excel at more than one thing. **18**

We believe each person comes to the ZCoB with the capacity to contribute and succeed. **19**

We believe strong relationships are key to our success. **20**

We believe we need our guests more than they need us. **21**

We believe our community is our terroir. **22**

We believe asking for help is a sign of strength. **23**

We believe we are stronger together (as a ZCoB with shared services) than apart (as fully independent businesses). **24**

We believe that a truly diverse workforce and an equitable, inclusive work culture maximize the greatest potential of our organization. **25**

We believe a diverse group makes better decisions. **26**

We believe business is a way to do good in the world. **27**

We believe good work can be one of the most fulfilling things one ever engages in. **28**

We believe in investing in future generations. **29**

We believe in learning, teaching, and lavishly sharing information. **30**

We believe small actions make a big difference. **31**

# of beliefs

We believe you really can taste the difference. **32**

We believe our choice of words makes a big difference. **33**

We believe in our tools and "trusting in the process." **34**

We believe visions of success lead to greatness. **35**

We believe in the effectiveness of open book management. **36**

We believe following the 3 Steps to Great Service and 5 Steps to Handling Complaints leads us to great service. **37**

We believe all three bottom lines are equally important. **38**

We believe in continuous improvement and ambitious goals that lead us to eliminate waste. **39**

We believe applying the spirit of generosity in every action benefits the business, everyone in it, and everyone we interact with. **40**

We believe the more people we involve in ownership, the more effective the organization will be, and the more we can better the lives of everyone who is part of the ZCoB. **41**

We believe profit is good because it allows us to continue to operate and gives us the means to shape the future in a positive way. **42**

We believe we're each 100% responsible for the health of the ZCoB, of which we're a part. **43**

We believe our organization will do best when everyone who works here is actively and intentionally contributing. **44**

We believe in Servant Leadership and Stewardship. **45**

We believe everyone is responsible for leadership. **46**

We believe humility is an essential ingredient for effective leadership and contributes to personal growth and success. **47**

We believe leading with positive beliefs makes a positive difference.

**What it looks like when we're
IN ALIGNMENT**

Acknowledging that all human beings have beliefs about almost everything.

We embrace that we all have the freedom to choose what we believe.

We understand, though difficult, we all have the ability to change what we believe.

We know that if our beliefs are not aligned with our vision/preferred future/desired outcomes we will not succeed.

We know that choosing positive beliefs creates the sort of healthy, positive organization we're after.

Understanding that we each have a long list of beliefs that we bring with us from past life experiences.

By leading with positive beliefs we create the kind of positive outcomes we're committed to attaining.

We have positive beliefs about our ability to deal with challenges.

**What it looks like when we're
OUT OF ALIGNMENT**

We're unconscious of our beliefs.

We let our negative beliefs unconsciously influence our actions to the detriment of our collective work.

We believe that someone is going to fail, and don't take action to adjust course.

We believe our manager/staffer/coworker/partner/customer is a "jerk," "loser," etc.

We don't believe in what we're selling/making AND we choose not to address the issue by working to improve the item.

We believe that another part of our organization is doing a bad job but don't productively engage with them about the issue or work to help them succeed.

We believe customers or vendors are out to get us.

Zingerman's® STATEMENT OF BELIEFS

We believe each person is a creative, unique individual who can do great things in life.

What it looks like when we're IN ALIGNMENT

We respect the individuality of each member of the ZCoB.

We treat each ZCoBber as someone of great significance and as a present and future leader.

We encourage everyone to write a vision and pursue their dreams, wherever that takes them.

We work to minimize the impact of unconscious bias.

We take time to get to know each person we work with.

What it looks like when we're OUT OF ALIGNMENT

We speak about individuals or groups using "us versus them" language rather than by name.

We assign identities to individuals based on some component of their work or personal history.

We don't take the time to learn each other's stories.

We class people by groups rather than honoring their uniqueness ("you know how accountants are," etc.).

We make statements about how "everyone thinks X" or "no one does Y."

We make assumptions, stereotype, categorize, etc.

We believe our individual success can be assessed by how much we help those around us to develop and grow.

What it looks like when we're IN ALIGNMENT

We share credit liberally.

We have caring conversations when needed and stay with them until we reach understanding and an effective outcome.

We choose to believe the best about our coworkers.

When something's not going right, we choose positive beliefs and compassion, not blame.

We find ways to help our colleagues get to greatness by helping them build on their strengths and supporting them as best we can in areas of weakness.

What it looks like when we're OUT OF ALIGNMENT

We focus on our own success at the expense of others.

We find fault, rather finding ways to share good fortune.

We hold negative beliefs about others—"He's trying to sabotage me." "She's not committed to quality." "He doesn't care about the organization."

When performance is falling short, we focus on that—the quality of work done—not on negative beliefs.

Zingerman's® STATEMENT OF BELIEFS

We believe personal transformation and growth are imperative to our personal and organizational success.

What it looks like when we're IN ALIGNMENT

We give people second chances.

We invest in learnings such as University of Zingerman's (UofZ) and Leadership Development Program (LDP) and business books.

We encourage everyone here to write a personal/work vision and then work with them to craft it, agree on it and help implement it. And we're willing to spend time to talk through those draft visions, refine them and work to help implement them.

We encourage each other to push out of our "comfort zones" and into the "learning zone."

We're compassionate in our interactions.

We commit to helping everyone here get to greatness, understanding that their pace and preferred path might not be the same as our own.

What it looks like when we're OUT OF ALIGNMENT

We freeze people in time.

We fail to invest in training and staff development.

We fall into perfectionism.

We allow ourselves to stand pat rather than pushing ourselves toward continuous improvement.

We "write people off," believing that "they'll never get to success."

We allow our discomfort to dominate relationships rather than working together to get past it.

We believe everyone can excel at more than one thing.

What it looks like when we're IN ALIGNMENT

We support each other's 1 + 1 work.

We post jobs so people can apply for new areas of focus.

We regularly work to crosstrain.

We teach our internal classes to everyone—you don't need to work in a particular area to learn about it.

We give internal scholarships every year for ZCoBbers who want to learn about new topics and bring their learning back to the ZCoB.

What it looks like when we're OUT OF ALIGNMENT

We limit people's decision making and involvement to those tasks directly related to their jobs.

We don't ask for input from others who might be outside the immediate range of influence on an issue.

We limit training to those who might learn from it even though it's "not their job."

We rule out scholarship candidates because they want to pursue learning "outside their current field" of work.

Zingerman's® STATEMENT OF BELIEFS

We believe each person comes to the ZCoB with the capacity to contribute and succeed.

What it looks like when we're IN ALIGNMENT

We look for insight from and honor the input of every member of the organization.

We listen well to what's in each person's heart and head and do our best to understand where our colleagues are coming from.

We actively engage everyone in the ZCoB—big issues, small issues, and everything in between—we believe that everyone has interesting insight to offer.

We encourage everyone here to write a personal/work vision and then work with them to craft it, get alignment on it and help implement it.

We use our Bottom-Line Change process which is, by definition, inclusive.

What it looks like when we're OUT OF ALIGNMENT

We exclude people from decisions and miss opportunities to find creative solutions.

We move to decisions in a management level conversation without taking time to involve others.

We skip over using Bottom-Line Change.

We believe strong relationships are key to our success.

What it looks like when we're
IN ALIGNMENT

We look for opportunities for people to connect across businesses.

We build connections with our community, past employees, and vendors.

People leave the organization (or no longer supply us) with grace and dignity, and are welcomed back into the businesses after they've left.

We follow through effectively on commitments we make to each other.

We respond in a timely way to phone calls, texts, emails and other enquiries.

We continue to act professionally with vendors, staff, customers, etc. even after they no longer work with us.

What it looks like when we're
OUT OF ALIGNMENT

We end relationships in anger and hold on to resentments.

We don't follow through on commitments or respond in a timely manner to requests.

We write people off rather than work together to get through awkwardness or discomfort.

We tie the quality of the relationship to people's job title or position.

We allow disagreements over tactics to get in the way of the way of the relationship.

We believe we need our guests more than they need us.

What it looks like when we're IN ALIGNMENT

We actively set out to honor our guests and earn their trust with every interaction.

We don't take any customer interaction for granted. We go out and re-earn our customers' trust every day.

We're regularly coming up with new strategic initiatives to differentiate ourselves in the marketplace.

What it looks like when we're OUT OF ALIGNMENT

We take our regulars for granted.

We start leading with "no" because we're worried a "yes" will be inconvenient or annoying.

When there's an out of the ordinary request from a guest we turn it down without first thinking about how we might make it happen and make someone's day in the process.

We believe our community is our terroir.

What it looks like when we're IN ALIGNMENT

Zingerman's is an Ann Arbor area institution and being present in the community develops a deep cultural connection so that the community is invested in our success.

The community is richer—culturally, spiritually, financially—because of our presence; and our personality and culture are informed by our being rooted in the "soil" of Ann Arbor. Coming to Ann Arbor, for many food lovers, means a trip to Zingerman's.

The decision to stay here and not open further afield is a meaningful differentiator for us in the marketplace.

We connect staff across the ZCoB businesses and with other parts of our community.

What it looks like when we're OUT OF ALIGNMENT

We spend time and energy thinking about the fact that we are missing opportunities for us to open elsewhere.

We miss opportunities for building meaningful connections to Ann Arbor in new and different ways.

We believe asking for help is a sign of strength.

What it looks like when we're IN ALIGNMENT

We acknowledge when we need help and/or when we're in over our head.

We encourage people to ask for help, and appreciate them when they do it.

We all make a point of acknowledging strength, experience, and insight in others in the organization.

We regularly tell stories of times where we asked for help and also of times where we failed to do but later realized it would have been the right thing to do.

What it looks like when we're OUT OF ALIGNMENT

We make mistakes because we're in over our heads without having asked for support and assistance from others

We fail to ask for outside input.

We get annoyed when someone asks us for help.

When a coworker asks for help we respond with frustration, telling them—directly or indirectly—that they should have been able to handle it on their own.

We believe we are stronger together (as a ZCoB with some shared services) than apart (as fully independent businesses).

What it looks like when we're IN ALIGNMENT

We celebrate the success of one business as success for the whole.

We promote each other's businesses, products, services, and secret specials.

We talk about each other's ZCoB businesses as we do our own.

We regularly revisit what those services are and make adjustments accordingly.

What it looks like when we're OUT OF ALIGNMENT

We make decisions without considering the effect on other businesses.

We talk negatively about each other.

We focus on who is holding us back, rather than leading the way forward.

In marketing work we focus exclusively on our business and pass up opportunities to connect and promote across the ZCoB.

We believe that a truly diverse workforce and an equitable, inclusive work culture maximize the greatest potential of our organization.

What it looks like when we're IN ALIGNMENT

Our recruitment is diverse and referrals received from the outside are diverse because we are known to value and seek diversity.

People who are not in the majority feel especially valued and respected.

There is significant diversity at all leadership levels of the organization.

The path to promotion is clear and made accessible to all.

People who are not in the majority feel sufficiently safe to set healthy boundaries and can bring their full selves to work every day.

Everyone is equally held accountable.

Uncomfortable moments are acknowledged and addressed in the moment.

The diversity class is seen as a valuable learning opportunity for everyone and the content is internalized and evidenced as operational.

What it looks like when we're OUT OF ALIGNMENT

The applicant pool is not diverse because diverse folks do not choose to apply and don't want to work with us.

People who are not in the majority do not feel valued or respected based on their gender, class, ethnicity or racial identities.

There is no diversity or minimal diversity at the high leadership levels.

The route to promotion is not clearly understood and is not a path made equally accessible to all.

People who are not in the majority are afraid to speak up for fear of retribution or marginalization.

Not everyone is equally held accountable.

Uncomfortable moments are laughed off or ignored.

The diversity class has little impact on personal transformation or behavior at work and is treated as a passport requirement to be checked off.

We believe a diverse group makes better decisions.

What it looks like when we're IN ALIGNMENT

We hold open meetings.

We actively work to include folks of varying backgrounds in all our work.

We make time to reach out to engage ZCoBbers from often under-represented groups.

Those who are already included take responsibility to include those who aren't yet.

We actively work to build a diverse and inclusive organization at every level.

People share their stories to make our collective culture stronger.

We follow our BLC process.

We work to share ethical challenges in constructive and appropriate ways.

We regularly reach outside the ZCoB to tap other perspectives.

What it looks like when we're OUT OF ALIGNMENT

We fail to include those from elsewhere in the organization.

We forget how overwhelming it is to be new or to feel different.

We allow unconscious biases to get in the way of doing inclusive work.

We keep conversations in our own "group," rather than reach out to hear other perspectives.

We don't solicit input from people outside the ZCoB who have valuable insight.

We don't make time for one on one conversations to hear other people's perspectives.

Zingerman's ® STATEMENT OF BELIEFS

We believe business is a way to do good in the world.

What it looks like when we're IN ALIGNMENT

We generate profit to improve our businesses, our community and the lives of the people who work here though gain share, community giving, community chest.

We leave everyone and everything we interact with better than when we first came into contact—staff, customers, the community, vendors, and the environment.

What it looks like when we're OUT OF ALIGNMENT

We allow the financial bottom line to suffer in a decision.

We fail to think through the larger impact of our decisions.

We don't act in alignment with the spirit of generosity.

We think only about our own small part of the ecosystem we're in, rather than approaching our work with a big picture and long term perspective.

We believe good work can be one of the most fulfilling things one ever engages in.

What it looks like when we're IN ALIGNMENT

We figure out how to make working here ever more rewarding for all involved.

We help everyone here pursue their dreams where possible within the ZCoB—and if not in the ZCoB, we give them our support as best we can anyways.

We work to engage meaningfully with every staff member.

We offer a lot of opportunity for growth and advancement such as 1+1 work, job postings, vision writing, education, etc.

We work hard to learn about each other's hopes and dreams and then support each other in going after them.

What it looks like when we're OUT OF ALIGNMENT

We leave people mostly to do their "jobs" without engaging them fully.

Work becomes a burden.

We show up only because we "have to."

Our energy is disengaged and cynical.

We assign people tasks and train them only on "how-tos" but forget to share the "Why" behind what we're doing.

We fail to show staff how their work is having an impact and making a positive difference in the world.

We believe in investing in future generations.

What it looks like when we're IN ALIGNMENT

We continuously work to reduce waste.

We put time, money, and effort into properly recycling, composting, and significantly reducing our carbon footprint.

We take time to plan so we can sustain our businesses and the ZCoB for generations.

We help our vendors to sustain their businesses and traditional food for generations.

What it looks like when we're OUT OF ALIGNMENT

We choose a less expensive option or easier way in the moment, regardless of future consequences.

We fail to recognize the power of our relationships with our vendors.

We make decisions without weighing the importance of impacts in the future.

We let short-term fixes drive our decisions without considering root causes and long-term vision.

We believe in learning, teaching, and lavishly sharing information.

What it looks like when we're IN ALIGNMENT

The more we learn the better we do.

The more we teach the better we learn.

What people learn at work can improve their personal lives as well.

We err on the side of over-communication.

We share notes from our meetings throughout the organization.

We keep most of our meetings open (allowing for private HR issues, crisis management, or conversations that really call for a smaller group).

We use Bottom Line Change to make large and small organizational changes.

We have a library of resources available to all.

We share social and intellectual capital generously.

We share sources inside and outside the ZCoB liberally.

What it looks like when we're OUT OF ALIGNMENT

We withhold information and resources from each other.

We assume that others already know things.

We operate with the belief that people don't "need to know."

We restrict training to only those who "really need" it without thinking about their long term potential for development.

We start to close more and more meetings.

We hold our time and our information close to the vest rather than sharing liberally across our community.

We believe small actions make a big difference.

What it looks like when we're IN ALIGNMENT

We take time to appreciate each other for small actions that make a coworker's or guest's day.

We make small changes to our work, relationships, and food.

We give back to our community by volunteering hour by hour.

What it looks like when we're OUT OF ALIGNMENT

We wait for the perfect time to make a big, important sounding decision.

We focus on hierarchical values such as "best" and "biggest" rather than small and everyday actions.

We believe you really can taste the difference.

What it looks like when we're IN ALIGNMENT

We continuously taste and carefully assess our food for its full-flavored and traditional nature.

While not everyone will want to buy our food, we believe that anyone interested can taste the difference between what we offer and what is readily available in the marketplace. When we find there is no meaningful difference, we work to create one by raising our quality bar higher.

We stick to high quality ingredients and continually work to find better sources and then to improve our raw materials.

We share our learnings with our staff and customers.

What it looks like when we're OUT OF ALIGNMENT

We don't take the time to educate our staff and customers.

We take shortcuts with ingredients when we think no one will notice.

We assume someone won't be able to tell the difference because of their background, experience, age, etc.

We believe our choice of words makes a big difference.

What it looks like when we're IN ALIGNMENT

We use "we" instead of "I" when talking about our organization.

We focus on actions not attributes, behaviors rather than attitudes.

We tie the person to their behavior.

We work to make "I" statements rather than "you" statements.

We stay away from dramatic language.

We use a 5:1 ratio of positive to constructive criticism which is likely to lead to a healthy loving relationship.

We treat and talk about each other as the unique and important individuals we are.

We listen to understand and use the tool of dialogue when we are stuck.

What it looks like when we're OUT OF ALIGNMENT

We're insensitive to (often unintentional) slurs that lead people to feel demeaned or excluded.

Using "they" instead of "we."

Saying "I lied" or "I'm an idiot" rather than the more respectful-to-self statement, "I made a mistake."

Saying "managers do . . ." or "employees are . . ." (talking about groups as if they are all the same person).

We speak about "they," "everyone," "no one," "those people," etc.

We use "my" instead of "our" for collective work.

We judge people for their actions, rather than separating the person from the still critical performance.

We believe in our tools and "trusting in the process."

What it looks like when we're IN ALIGNMENT

We follow proven systems like Bottom-Line Change or agreed-upon SOPs even when, part-way through, it seems like things are not working.

We work through the ups and downs that go with making any long term meaningful change happen.

We learn, teach, and model our tools in our everyday work.

We examine our culture and our actions to make sure our systems are in line with our beliefs and new knowledge.

What it looks like when we're OUT OF ALIGNMENT

We skip steps of our recipes because they "take too long."

We give up on meaningful change too soon.

We skip over writing SOPs.

We don't follow SOPs.

When our recipes or SOPs are out of date, we just ignore them rather than doing the work to keep them current.

We believe visions of success lead to greatness.

What it looks like when we're IN ALIGNMENT

We write visions for projects, ourselves, our businesses.

We engage with and support the visions of others.

We actively work to implement; bringing visions to fruition.

We encourage everyone here to write a personal/work vision and then work with them to craft it, agree on it and help implement it.

We consistently start with the "what" and not the "how."

What it looks like when we're OUT OF ALIGNMENT

We start with the "how" and not the "what."

We start with strategy or tactics rather than vision.

We do extensive work on a project or change without having a vision for what success will look like.

We teach visioning only to a select few how really "need it" rather than sharing the process widely with every part of the ZCoB.

We believe in the effectiveness of open book management.

What it looks like when we're IN ALIGNMENT

We plan, we huddle, we forecast, we know and teach the rules.

We get as many people involved as possible involved in writing the annual plans.

We encourage new ZCoBbers to get involved in huddles ASAP.

We know our unit's numbers, talk about them regularly and consistently work to improve them.

We're all able to have fluid discussions about business and finance on a day to day level.

When we're struggling with a repetitive problem, we look to see how we can use open book to help understand and deal with it.

What it looks like when we're OUT OF ALIGNMENT

We create plans behind closed doors.

We don't check our progress.

We have conversations outside of our huddles that could happen in the open.

We slip away from having good rigor in our forecasting work.

We don't take and share notes from our huddles.

We don't hold ourselves accountable for tasks taken in huddles.

We believe following the 3 Steps to Great Service and 5 Steps to Handling Complaints leads us to great service.

What it looks like when we're IN ALIGNMENT

Following the 3 Steps and 5 Steps is a habit.

We consistently take each and every step.

We follow through when we fall short—using second person in, time lapse, exceptional extra miles, etc.

What it looks like when we're OUT OF ALIGNMENT

We don't follow the 10/4 rule.

We forget to go the extra mile for customers and coworkers.

We don't make problems right effectively.

We don't treat our coworkers with the same care and attention as we do customers.

We fail to handle complaints from coworkers.

We believe all three bottom lines are equally important.

What it looks like when we're IN ALIGNMENT

We carefully weigh each decision by considering its impact on each of our bottom lines.

We embrace the creative tension and conflict between all three bottom lines.

We actively measure all three bottom lines on our DORs.

We coach our staff on understanding all three.

What it looks like when we're OUT OF ALIGNMENT

We allow imbalance to go on for long periods of time without self-correcting.

We don't measure one as mindfully as another.

We exclude one of our bottom lines in our decision making.

We take shortcuts and focus on the one we're most comfortable with.

We believe in continuous improvement and ambitious goals that lead us to eliminate waste.

What it looks like when we're IN ALIGNMENT

We practice a scientific approach to our work.

We experiment and we use the collected facts and evidence to continuously improve and eliminate waste.

We're always working to improve our own work in self-management, knowledge or product and process, etc.

We use kata in all our businesses.

What it looks like when we're OUT OF ALIGNMENT

We avoid making a systems change because change is hard.

We don't test or experiment before we make a decision.

We settle for the status quo rather than challenging ourselves to grow and develop.

We believe applying the spirit of generosity in every action benefits the business, everyone in it, and everyone we interact with.

**What it looks like when we're
IN ALIGNMENT**

We believe that the success of other Zingerman's businesses, and other ZCoBbers, enhances our own success.

We take an abundance approach—there's enough for everyone.

When in doubt, we actively share more.

**What it looks like when we're
OUT OF ALIGNMENT**

We focus on why the success of others will reduce our sales or cause us harm.

We guard our resources to a fault.

We believe the more people we involve in ownership, the more effective the organization will be, and the more we can better the lives of everyone who is part of the ZCoB.

What it looks like when we're
IN ALIGNMENT

We provide Community Shares as a means of ownership.

Community Shareholders have a voice in organizational decision making.

We encourage more people to become Managing Partners.

There is a clear, documented path to becoming Managing Partner and Staff Partner.

What it looks like when we're
OUT OF ALIGNMENT

We restrict ownership to a chosen few.

We make it unnecessarily difficult to become an owner in the ZCoB.

We believe profit is good because it allows us to continue to operate and gives us the means to shape the future in a positive way.

**What it looks like when we're
IN ALIGNMENT**

With a healthy level of profit, the organization is sustainable.

5.1% target NOP.

We recognize and honor those who deliver healthy, ethically-based profits to the organization.

Our profits are rooted in our guiding principles and shared values.

Sharing profits, effectively and appropriately, is an essential part of our sustainable business.

**What it looks like when we're
OUT OF ALIGNMENT**

We don't hold ourselves accountable for being effectively profitable.

We continue to operate with little or no profit.

Zingerman's ® STATEMENT OF BELIEFS

We believe we're each 100% responsible for the health of the ZCoB, of which we're a part.

What it looks like when we're IN ALIGNMENT

We respectfully ask each other to honor our commitments. Those requests go across all lines of hierarchy or business.

Staff at all levels take responsibility for staff survey results and suggest ways to improve.

When we make a mistake we apologize and make it right in the moment.

When we see an opportunity for another department, business, or individual to grow and succeed we share the idea with them.

What it looks like when we're OUT OF ALIGNMENT

We avoid disciplining a staff member because it's awkward.

We don't hold each other accountable by setting creative consequences.

We don't go direct when we're frustrated with others in the ZCoB.

We blame bosses/staff/other businesses for our problems, rather than taking responsibility for leading the way to a better future.

We act helpless and blame others.

We believe our organization will do best when everyone who works here is actively and intentionally contributing.

What it looks like when we're IN ALIGNMENT

We give staff opportunities to make a difference and help each ZCoBber to understand the value/impact of every action taken.

From their first day on the job, we authorize staff members to do whatever they need to do for customers to deliver a great experience.

We encourage every staff member to get involved as much as possible.

Our meetings, classes and huddles are pretty much open to all.

We go out of our way to gently and caringly engage anyone who might feel excluded for any reason.

What it looks like when we're OUT OF ALIGNMENT

We've given up on an employee but allow them to continue to work here.

We leave people on the periphery without trying to get them to be more involved in running the ZCoB.

We don't share huddle notes widely.

We default to exclusion rather than inclusion.

Zingerman's® STATEMENT OF BELIEFS

We believe in Servant Leadership and Stewardship.

What it looks like when we're IN ALIGNMENT

We make decisions in the best interest of the organization.

We treat everyone with dignity and kindness.

We show love and care in all our actions.

We recognize we need our employees more than they need us.

The more responsibility we take, the more we serve (servant leadership).

We focus on, and deliver, great service to our co-workers as much as do for guests and clients.

Leaders treat staff like customers, using the 3 steps to great service and 5 steps to handling complaints.

We work through our frustrations with colleagues first, then talk with them from a place of calm.

What it looks like when we're OUT OF ALIGNMENT

We default to hierarchical management.

We start to act like staff are here to serve the leaders.

We treat staff members/coworkers rudely.

We fail to base our actions on what's best for the organization overall and instead focus mostly on what helps our direct group.

We don't negotiate meaningfully and respectfully through difficult issues.

We don't hold ourselves accountable for our commitments.

We act in unethical ways.

We drop our regular learning and teaching.

We believe everyone is responsible for leadership.

What it looks like when we're IN ALIGNMENT

Our committees and work groups are made up of a representation of all staff from multiple businesses, roles, education, tenure, and demographics.

Any staff member can lead a possible change using the BLC process.

It's everyone's responsibility to make things right for any guest.

Anyone can capture data to propose positive, effective change.

What it looks like when we're OUT OF ALIGNMENT

People waiting for someone else to make positive change.

Front-line staff feel like they have to go get a manager to get permission to make things right for a guest.

We talk down to colleagues.

We act on the belief that "the bosses" will figure it all out and everyone else should just wait for their directions.

We believe humility is an essential ingredient for effective leadership and contributes to personal growth and success.

What it looks like when we're IN ALIGNMENT

We share credit liberally.

We interview and hire with humility in mind.

We focus mostly on team success.

We trust and are able to learn from peers as a result of that trust.

What it looks like when we're OUT OF ALIGNMENT

Leaders forget to ask staff for input on decisions.

Staff are afraid to approach leaders when they're not in agreement with decisions.

We focus on heroes and villains rather than embracing that we're all flawed human beings trying to do the right thing.

reflections

Taking time to reflect on what we've learned has proven helpful to us in putting our training tools to work. Here are some questions to prompt some reflection on the Statement of Beliefs.

What surprised you?

What did you find most helpful?

What are you most excited about?

What area will you be the most challenged in?

What action steps will you take?

We believe, as noted on page 23, that asking for help is a sign of strength. Here are a few resources for when you need help:

- Your manager
- Your peers
- Partners
- *Staff Guide*
- D4P at ZingNet: 734.668.4662 d4p@zingermans.com
- Employee Assistance Program: 800.448.8326 LifeAdvisorEAP.com
- Read *Workin'*